**ANCIENT CIVILIZATIONS** Need to Know

SilverTip

# The Rise and Fall of Ancient China

by D. R. Faust

Consultant: Caitlin Krieck, Social Studies Teacher and Instructional Coach, The Lab School of Washington

**BEARPORT** PUBLISHING

Minneapolis, Minnesota

## Credits

Cover and title page, © rongyiquan/Shutterstock; 5, © Dana.S/Shutterstock; 7, © titoOnz/Shutterstock; 9, © Ian Winslow/Shutterstock; 11, © Chronicle/Alamy Stock Photo; 13, © Ma Lin /Wikimedia Commons; 15, © Shan_shan/Shutterstock; 17, © Philip Lange/Shutterstock; 18, © 兵馬俑博物館/Creative Commons Attribution-Share Alike 4.0 International; 19, © Yuangeng Zhang/Shutterstock; 23, © NPM/Wikimedia Commons; 24, © SmallJarsWithGreenLabels/Creative Commons Attribution-Share Alike 4.0 International; 25, © CPA Media Pte Ltd /Alamy Stock Photo; 27, © Public Domain/Wikipedia; 28a, © Shan_shan/Shutterstock; 28b, © Philip Lange/Shutterstock; 28c, © Public Domain/Wikimedia Commons; 28d, © http://earlyworldhistory.blogspot.com/2012/03/liu-bang.html/Wikimedia Commons; 28e, © Public Domain/Wikipedia.

## Bearport Publishing Company Product Development Team

President: Jen Jenson; Director of Product Development: Spencer Brinker; Managing Editor: Allison Juda; Associate Editor: Naomi Reich; Associate Editor: Tiana Tran; Art Director: Colin O'Dea; Designer: Kim Jones; Designer: Kayla Eggert; Product Development Assistant: Owen Hamlin

## Statement on Usage of Generative Artificial Intelligence

Bearport Publishing remains committed to publishing high-quality nonfiction books. Therefore, we restrict the use of generative AI to ensure accuracy of all text and visual components pertaining to a book's subject. See BearportPublishing.com for details.

*Library of Congress Cataloging-in-Publication Data*

Names: Faust, Daniel R., author.
Title: The rise and fall of ancient China / by D.R. Faust.
Description: Minneapolis, Minnesota : Bearport Publishing Company, [2025] |
  Series: Ancient civilizations : need to know | Silvertip books. |
  Includes bibliographical references and index.
Identifiers: LCCN 2023059643 (print) | LCCN 2023059644 (ebook) | ISBN
  9798892320429 (library binding) | ISBN 9798892325165 (paperback) | ISBN
  9798892321754 (ebook)
Subjects: LCSH: China—Civilization—To 221 B.C.—Juvenile literature. |
  China—Civilization—221 B.C.-960 A.D.—Juvenile literature.
Classification: LCC DS741.65 .F39 2025  (print) | LCC DS741.65  (ebook) |
  DDC 931—dc23/eng/20240126
LC record available at https://lccn.loc.gov/2023059643
LC ebook record available at https://lccn.loc.gov/2023059644

Copyright © 2025 Bearport Publishing Company. All rights reserved. No part of this publication may be reproduced in whole or in part, stored in any retrieval system, or transmitted in any form or by any means, electronic, mechanical, photocopying, recording, or otherwise, without written permission from the publisher. Bearport Publishing is a division of Chrysalis Education Group.

For more information, write to Bearport Publishing, 5357 Penn Avenue South, Minneapolis, MN 55419.

# Contents

Past Meets Present . . . . . . . . . . . . . 4
Shaped by the Land . . . . . . . . . . . . 6
Before Ancient China . . . . . . . . . . . 10
The Rise of Dynasties . . . . . . . . . . 12
China's First Dynasties . . . . . . . . . 14
Fighting for Power . . . . . . . . . . . . 18
The Chinese Empire . . . . . . . . . . . 20
A Growing Economy . . . . . . . . . . . 22
A Broken Empire . . . . . . . . . . . . . 26

Ancient China Timeline . . . . . . . . .28
SilverTips for Success . . . . . . . . . .29
Glossary . . . . . . . . . . . . . . . . . . . .30
Read More . . . . . . . . . . . . . . . . . .31
Learn More Online . . . . . . . . . . . .31
Index . . . . . . . . . . . . . . . . . . . . . . .32
About the Author . . . . . . . . . . . . .32

# Past Meets Present

Have you ever watched fireworks light up the sky? How about used a piece of paper? These important inventions came from ancient China. Its **civilization** started as far back as 1600 BCE. But this China of the past still impacts our lives today.

> The first fireworks were bamboo tubes filled with gunpowder. Paper was originally made from old rags. Over time, paper makers started using plants instead.

# Shaped by the Land

China's geography has long kept it separate. The huge Asian country is surrounded by the Himalaya Mountains, the Gobi Desert, and the Pacific Ocean. These landforms allowed ancient China to develop without much **influence** from other countries. The harsh lands also protected China from **invaders**.

> The Himalayas stand along the southwest border of China. The mountain chain has some of the tallest peaks on Earth. Mount Everest is the tallest. It reaches heights of more than 29,000 feet (8,800 m).

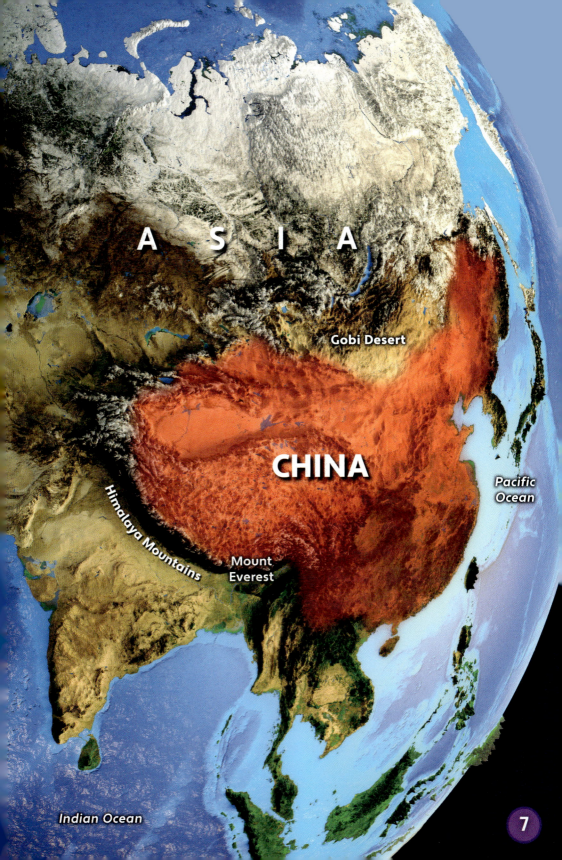

Two major rivers were also important in shaping China's history. Huang He, or the Yellow River, is in the north. The Yangtze River can be found in the south.

Both rivers were good for fishing. Regular river flooding made the soil good for farming. China's first villages were built along these rivers.

> The Yellow River is shorter than the Yangtze. However, it is still one of the longest river systems in the world. The Yellow River Valley is widely thought of as the birthplace of Chinese civilization.

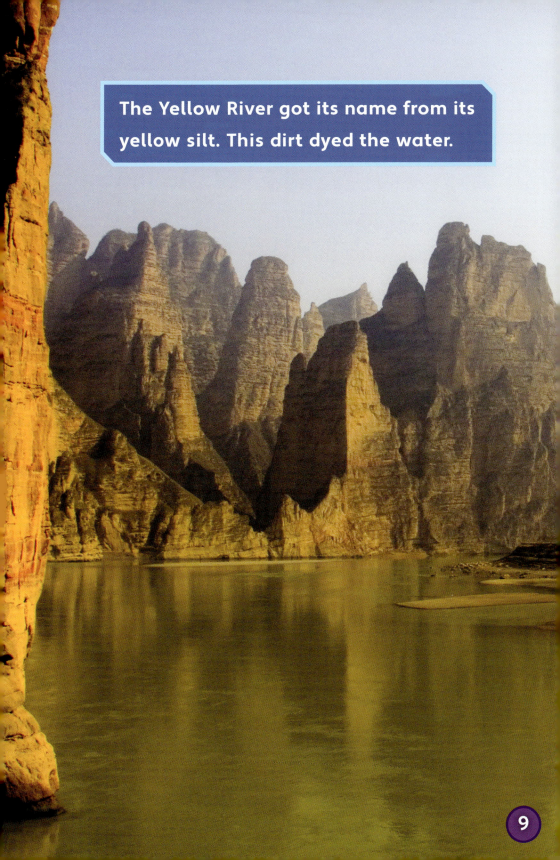
The Yellow River got its name from its yellow silt. This dirt dyed the water.

# Before Ancient China

China has one of the oldest civilizations in the world. Humans have lived there for about 80,000 years. Before the period we call ancient China, there were many different kingdoms. They ruled different parts of the land.

**Legends** say that the earliest kingdoms in China were ruled by godlike beings. They were called the Three **Sovereigns** and the Five **Emperors**.

The Yellow Emperor, one of the Five Emperors

# The Rise of Dynasties

Ancient China was shaped by dynasties. A series of rulers from the same family would lead the country for a period of time. Sons would take control from fathers. Some dynasties lasted only a few years. Others stretched for hundreds. Each one left a unique mark.

> Some people say the Xia was the first dynasty of China. Others disagree. They think the Xia dynasty was just a legend.

Yu the Great

The Xia dynasty was said to be started by Yu the Great.

# China's First Dynasties

The Shang was the first confirmed dynasty in China. Shang rulers were in power from about 1600 to 1046 BCE.

The Shang dynasty set up government systems. They made a 360-day calendar. This dynasty also saw the first Chinese writing.

> The Shang were the first to have written records. These historical writings had information about the marriages and deaths of rulers. They also noted important battles and natural disasters.

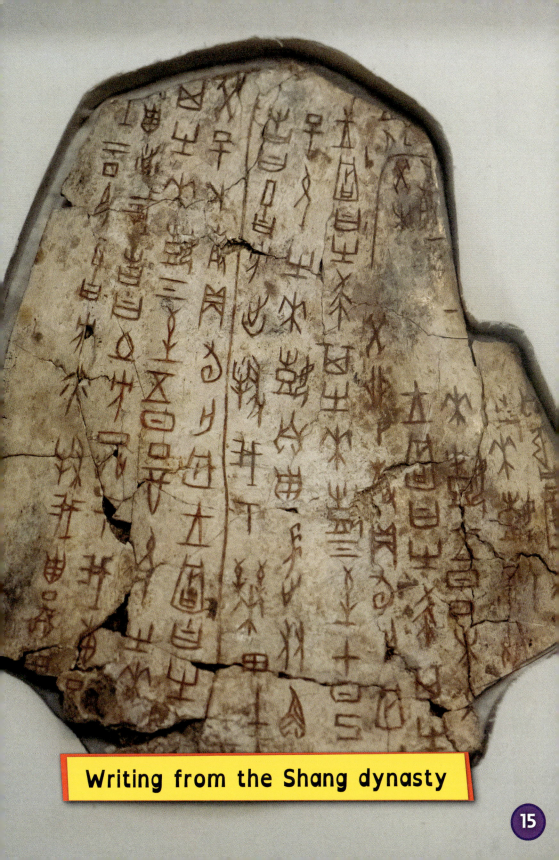
Writing from the Shang dynasty

The Shang dynasty was followed by the Zhou. This was the longest-running ancient dynasty. The Zhou dynasty had some of ancient China's most famous thinkers. Confucius was a Chinese **philosopher**. His teachings were turned into a way of life. The first writings of Taoism also came during the Zhou dynasty.

> The Zhou dynasty was divided into two eras. The Western Zhou was first. During this time, the capital was in a western city. Then, the capital moved east. This time was called the Eastern Zhou era.

Confucius

# Fighting for Power

Near the end of the Zhou dynasty, China broke into several smaller states. Each wanted power. Seven major groups and a few smaller ones fought for control. This time was called the Warring States period. Many groups built walls to keep out unfriendly invaders.

The fighting during this time led to the invention of new weapons. People started making stronger weapons out of iron and steel. They invented the crossbow to shoot arrows at their enemies.

# The Chinese Empire

Eventually, the Warring States period ended. China came together under the Qin dynasty in 221 BCE. Though this dynasty did not last long, it united China into an empire. The country was ruled by a single leader called an emperor. The Qin set up government systems that would be used for 2,000 years.

> The Qin emperor, Ying Zheng, set the same writing and measurement systems across all of China. He also started connecting walls and forts from the Warring States period. They would become the Great Wall of China.

# A Growing Economy

Next came the Han dynasty. During this time from 206 BCE to 220 CE, China saw a period of **stability** and advancement. The Han made a system of laws and improved education. There was a lot of growth in the Chinese **economy**.

> The Han dynasty was responsible for much of the Chinese culture still around today. In fact, *Han* became the Chinese word for people who are from China.

Liu Bang, also known as the Gazou emperor, started the Han dynasty.

During this time, there were many advances in sailing and shipbuilding. This helped China trade with its neighbors.

The ancient Chinese sent tea, spices, and expensive silk fabric to other countries. In return, they got wool, gold, and silver.

Traders traveled over land and sea. Their paths came to be called the Silk Road. This connected China with other countries in Asia, the Middle East, Africa, and Europe.

# A Broken Empire

After a series of weak rulers, the Han dynasty ended. China broke apart into smaller kingdoms again. These groups fought one another for control. Each tried to start its own dynasty. But none would ever be as powerful as the Han dynasty. It was the end of a united, powerful ancient China.

After the Han dynasty ended, China became weak. It was invaded by the Mongols. The Mongols controlled a lot of Asia and Europe for the next several centuries.

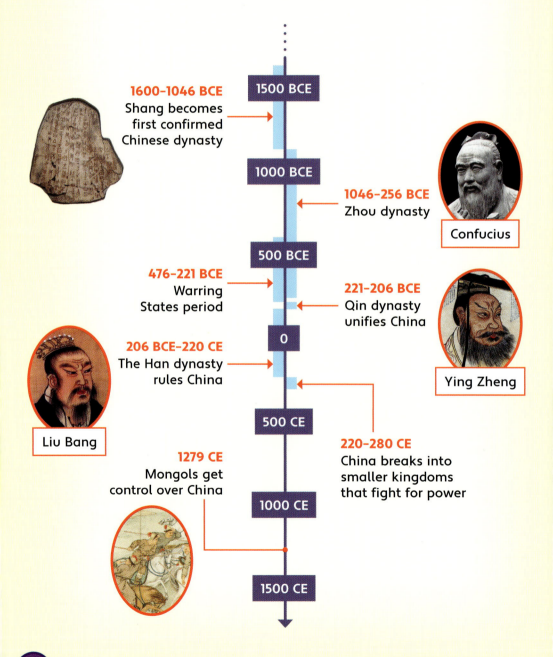

# SilverTips for SUCCESS

## ★ SilverTips for REVIEW

Review what you've learned. Use the text to help you.

### Define key terms

- dynasty
- empire
- Great Wall of China
- Silk Road
- Warring States period

### Check for understanding

How did geography shape the history of China?

What are dynasties in ancient China, and why were they important?

Name one of the major dynasties and a key achievement of this era.

### Think deeper

Which dynasty do you think had the most impact on making China into the country we know today and why?

## ★ SilverTips on TEST-TAKING

- **Make a study plan.** Ask your teacher what the test is going to cover. Then, set aside time to study a little bit every day.
- **Read all the questions carefully.** Be sure you know what is being asked.
- **Skip any questions** you don't know how to answer right away. Mark them and come back later if you have time.

# Glossary

**civilization** a large group of people who share the same history and way of life

**dynasties** groups of rulers from the same family whose periods of control over ancient China mark the passage of time

**economy** financial activity

**emperors** rulers that control a group of countries or regions called an empire, with one leader at a time

**influence** impact on a large number of people

**invaders** people who enter a place by force in order to take it over

**legends** stories handed down from long ago that are often based on some facts but cannot be proven

**philosopher** a person who studies the nature of knowledge, reality, and life

**sovereigns** people or groups who have total power over a group or region

**stability** calmness and order without a lot of change

# Read More

**Andrews, Elizabeth.** *The Ancient Chinese (Ancient Civilizations).* Minneapolis: Pop!, 2023.

**Lawrence, Blythe.** *Great Wall of China (Structural Wonders).* Lake Elmo, MN: Focus Readers, 2023.

**Reynolds, Donna.** *Ancient China Revealed (Unearthing Ancient Civilizations).* New York: Cavendish Square Publishing, 2023.

# Learn More Online

1. Go to **www.factsurfer.com** or scan the QR code below.

2. Enter "**Civilizations Ancient China**" into the search box.

3. Click on the cover of this book to see a list of websites.

# Index

**Chinese empire** 20

**government** 14, 20

**Han dynasty** 22–23, 26, 28

**Himalaya Mountains** 6–7

**inventions** 4, 18

**legends** 10, 12

**philosophers** 16

**Qin dynasty** 20–21, 28

**Shang dynasty** 14–16, 28

**trade** 24

**Warring States period** 18, 20, 28

**Xia dynasty** 12–13

**Yangtze River** 8

**Yellow River** 8–9

**Zhou dynasty** 16, 18, 28

# About the Author

D. R. Faust is a freelance writer of fiction and nonfiction. They live in Queens, NY.